T0168013

DEBUNKING CREATION MYTHS ABOUT AMERICA'S PUBLIC LANDS

DEBUNKING CREATION MYTHS ABOUT AMERICA'S PUBLIC LANDS

John D. Leshy

THE UNIVERSITY OF UTAH PRESS

Salt Lake City

Publication of this keepsake edition is made possible in part by The Wallace Stegner
Center for Land, Resources and the Environment
S.J. Quinney College of Law
and by
The Special Collections Department
J. Willard Marriott Library

This lecture was originally delivered on March 14, 2018, at the 23rd annual symposium of
the Wallace Stegner Center for Land, Resources and the Environment.

 The Defiance House Man colophon is a registered trademark of The University
of Utah Press. It is based on a four-foot-tall Ancient Puebloan pictograph (late
PIII) near Glen Canyon, Utah.

COVER PHOTO AND FRONTISPIECE: Road Canyon, Bears Ears National Monument.
Photo by Bob Wick, Bureau of Land Management.

Printed and bound in the United States of America.

FOREWORD

The Wallace Stegner Lecture serves as a public forum for addressing the critical environmental issues that confront society. Conceived in 2009 on the centennial of Wallace Stegner's birth, the lecture honors the Pulitzer prize–winning author, educator, and conservationist by bringing a prominent scholar, public official, advocate, or spokesperson to the University of Utah with the aim of informing and promoting public dialogue over the relationship between humankind and the natural world. The lecture is delivered in connection with the Wallace Stegner Center's annual symposium and published by the University of Utah Press to ensure broad distribution. Just as Wallace Stegner envisioned a more just and sustainable world, the lecture acknowledges Stegner's enduring conservation legacy by giving voice to "the geography of hope" that he evoked so eloquently throughout his distinguished career.

The 2018 Wallace Stegner Lecture was delivered by Professor John D. Leshy on the subject of "Debunking Creation Myths about America's Public Lands." Controversy over public land ownership and management has been a constant ever since the federal government began acquiring large landholdings. Professor Leshy, drawing upon original historical research, reexamines the purposes and policies behind federal land ownership, explaining how national policy has long embraced federal ownership and conservation-oriented management policies. His conclusions offer important new insights into the recurrent effort to transfer the federal lands into state or private hands, and will certainly inform future debate on this matter.

Robert B. Keiter, Director
WALLACE STEGNER CENTER FOR LAND,
RESOURCES AND THE ENVIRONMENT

DEBUNKING CREATION MYTHS ABOUT AMERICA'S PUBLIC LANDS

I could not have conceived of a better occasion or venue for my remarks today. Wallace Stegner was one of America's greatest communicators about public lands and what they have meant to the nation, and Utah is currently where the most lively political discussions are found about their future.

There is no standard definition, legal or otherwise, for the term "public lands."[1] I use it to mean those lands owned by the U.S. that are generally open to the public and managed for broad public purposes. They are overseen by four federal agencies—the National Park Service, the U.S. Forest Service, the Fish and Wildlife Service, and the Bureau of Land Management. They carry many labels, including national parks, forests, wildlife refuges, monuments, wilderness areas, recreation areas, and conservation areas.[2]

When I first began dealing with public lands nearly a half-century ago, I—like most Americans—had no idea that the U.S. owned about 30 percent of the nation's land, more than six hundred million acres.

Even more noteworthy is this: while some of that vast acreage has been drilled and mined and dammed and logged and grazed by private interests, its chief worth to the nation today is first, to offer experiences in nature for recreation, inspiration, and scientific study; and second, to protect watersheds, wildlife, and other natural values.[3]

If you are, like me, interested in American political history, you might wonder how it was that the U.S. came to own and to manage such vast landholdings for such broad purposes. That outcome seems particularly noteworthy, considering that America's political

I appreciate the helpful suggestions on earlier drafts by Margaret Karp, Matt Lee-Ashley, Bruce Babbitt, Ralph Becker, Bill deBuys, Bill Hedden, Bob Keiter, John Ruple, Charles Wilkinson, Chris Wood, and, with figure 16, Lesley King. Errors are mine.

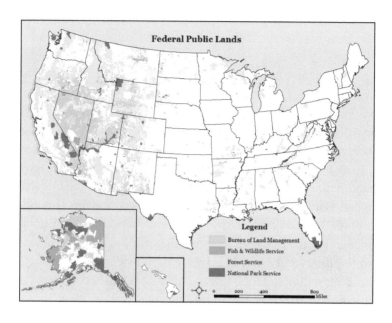

1. U.S. public lands, by agency (Source: Kara Clauser/Center for Biological Diversity).

Federal Agency Land Holdings (2014)

- **Bureau of Land Management (BLM)**   248 million acres

- **U.S. Forest Service**   193 million acres

- **U.S. Fish & Wildlife Service**   89 million acres

- **National Park Service**   80 million acres

- **TOTAL**   610 million acres

2. Total landholdings of each major federal land management agency.

culture has long extolled private property and regarded government—particularly the national government—with much wariness.

Discussions of public lands often tend to focus on their rich history, which is thoroughly intertwined with the nation's history. In recent years, I've been diving deeply into that history. I've become convinced that many commonly accepted ideas about this history do not reflect what really happened. They are, in a word, myths.

These myths have been influential, and not in a constructive way, in modern discussions of public land policy. Indeed, they have, I believe, been a major contributing factor to the polarization that too often characterizes those discussions.

The more they are understood to be myths, I believe, the more productive discussions could be about the future of public lands. I hope to debunk these myths here.

This task requires a quick tour of nearly two and a half centuries, so saddle up and hang onto your hats![4]

While public lands are not a topic most Americans think much about, sometimes they do grab national attention, as when in 2017 President Trump downsized the Bears Ears and Grand Staircase–Escalante National Monuments in Utah, and the year before when a ragtag milita group staged an armed takeover of Malheur National Wildlife Refuge in Oregon, spouting claims that the U.S. has no constitutional right to own these lands. Similar claims have been advanced by a team of lawyers hired by the state of Utah.[5]

One might conclude from such episodes that America's public lands have been a constant source of polarization, a kind of centrifugal force that drives Americans apart.

This is the first myth I want to debunk today.

The truth is that, over the nation's long history, the public lands have nearly always served to unify the country, not divide it.

That was demonstrated right at the beginning, in 1776, when the thirteen colonies declared their independence from the British and immediately set about creating a governing structure to establish

WESTERN LAND CLAIMS CEDED BY THE STATES

3. Western land claims ceded to the United States by seven of the original states (Source: Kmusser [CC BY-SA 2.5 (https://creativecommons.org/licenses/by-sa/2.5)], from Wikimedia Commons).

a national union of states. What was called the Articles of Confederation was sent to the thirteen former colonies for their ratification a few weeks after the Declaration of Independence. It required approval of every one of the thirteen former colonies before it could take effect. But ratification did not occur for almost five years, until 1781, shortly before the British surrender at Yorktown effectively ended the Revolutionary War. The aspiring nation, in other words, operated without a formally constituted government almost the entire time it was fighting to establish its independence.

The cause of this long delay? A dispute among the former colonies over claims to a vast amount of land between the crest of the

Appalachian Mountains and the Mississippi River. Specifically, the colonial charters of seven of the thirteen states-to-be defined their western boundaries in the vaguest of terms, which gave them somewhat overlapping claims to these western lands.

Six states-to-be, including Maryland, had fixed western boundaries. They feared they would be dominated by the other seven, whose power over western lands could well control the nation's destiny. Maryland refused to ratify the Articles of Confederation until those seven with western land claims agreed to yield them to the nation.

The argument of Maryland and its allies was simple: those western lands were being secured by the Revolutionary War sacrifices of lives and resources—or as they put it, the "blood and treasure"—of *all* the states. Those lands should, therefore, be administered for the common benefit of the entire country. The only way to guarantee that was for the national government to take ownership and control of them.

This argument eventually won out. The seven colonies with western land claims agreed to cede them to the new national government and, as a result, the United States came to own more than 230 million acres of land, or nearly half the real estate within its borders. In return, Maryland ratified the Articles of Confederation. Only then, as historian Richard Morris has reminded us, did the thirteen former colonies become states in a new national union, because it was the Articles creating the United States that "brought them into being."[6]

In this way the nation's public lands were, in fact, foundational to the nation.

It fairly quickly became apparent that the Articles of Confederation had some huge flaws, most notably in not giving the national government enough governing power. As a result, the U.S. Constitution was drafted in 1787 and ratified soon thereafter. Part of its strengthening of national authority was its so-called property clause. Adopted without controversy, it gave Congress authority to "make all needful rules and regulations regarding" these lands and other property "belonging to the United States."

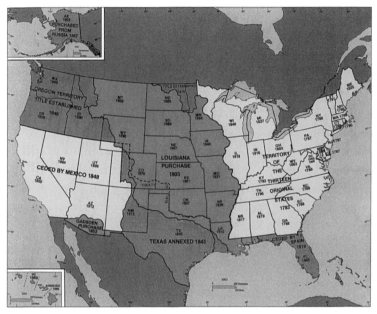

4. Territorial acquisitions of the U.S. (Source: National Atlas of the United States).

Over the next three-quarters of a century, public lands would remain key to U.S. expansion across the continent. The national government eventually came into ownership of more than 1.5 billion acres of land, through acquisitions from foreign governments, beginning with the Louisiana Purchase in 1803, and through its resolution of Native American land rights. How the U.S. acquired clear title to these lands from foreign governments and from tribes is a complicated story and, especially where Indians are concerned, certainly one with a dark side. But it took place largely in advance of, and separate from, the movement to keep significant amounts of public land permanently in U.S. ownership.

A second myth about public lands history is that the nation's founding generation expected new states would, upon their admission to the Union, become entitled to own the public lands the national government held within their borders.

This myth is at the core of the argument made by lawyers hired by the state of Utah and their fellow travelers.

Not a shred of historical evidence supports it.

What America's founding generation did generally expect was that Congress would adopt policies aimed at settling western public lands with people friendly to the U.S. and eventually would admit them as new states. The immediate goal was, understandably, to keep the nation together as settlement advanced across the continent. Particularly in the country's first decades, when national unity was fragile, this was hardly a sure thing.

But practically no one then advanced the idea that new states had some sort of claim, equitable or constitutional, to gain title to the public lands within their borders simply by virtue of their being admitted to the Union. Indeed, the question was never raised in political discussions in or out of Congress until nearly a half-century after the Declaration of Independence.

When it was put forward in the late 1820s by a few politicians in some of the newer states (but not, significantly, in territories aspiring to be states), the claim fell on deaf ears. Leaders across the political spectrum—from James Madison to Henry Clay, Andrew Jackson, and John C. Calhoun—were absolutely opposed to the notion of ceding all public lands to newly admitted states. On the floor of Congress, the idea was roundly condemned in the strongest terms, with members calling it "preposterous," "grasping," "one of the most extravagant pretensions that could possibly be urged," "absolute heresy," and "against the Constitution, against reason, and against right."[7]

The harsh political reaction was perfectly understandable. Members of Congress were chosen by voters in existing states. Simply ceding public lands to new states did not acknowledge that it was the "blood and treasure" of existing states that had been expended to acquire these lands from foreign governments and Indian tribes. Territorial interests seeking statehood were almost always regarded merely as supplicants, ever more so as the nation grew stronger and its control of its territory grew more secure. Had aspiring states demanded title to all public lands, their greed would have fatally undermined their case for statehood, and everyone involved knew it.[8]

This political dynamic never changed over time.

To drive the point home, Congress almost always required new states—including Utah—to agree, as a condition of being admitted into the Union, to formally pledge not to interfere with U.S. control of its public lands lying within their borders.[9]

A third myth is that, in the nation's first several decades, the public lands were viewed solely as an economic asset, to be sold to generate money primarily to pay off Revolutionary War debts.

This is associated with the previous myth, put forth to suggest that the founding generation had a limited vision of the role of public lands in building the nation.

Again the facts are to the contrary. From the beginning, Congress saw the public lands as far more than a cash cow. It saw them as a tool to achieve broad national policy objectives.

With tariffs generating most revenue for the Treasury, Congress gave away many more public lands than it sold, but attached various conditions to its gifts to advance these policies.

For example, it gave most newly admitted states generous grants of public lands, but on the condition that the land and revenues derived from them be used to create a system of common schools. This was a remarkably visionary step at a time when public education was practically unknown outside a few places in New England. These grants got larger over time. Originally, they comprised less than 3 percent of a new state's area, but by the time Utah was admitted in 1896, the school land grants comprised almost 11 percent of the lands within its borders.

Similarly, starting in 1862, Congress gave all states, old and new, rights to some of the nation's public lands on the condition that they be converted into an endowment to establish and sustain so-called "land grant" colleges. That gift of public lands led to some of the nation's most important institutions of higher learning, including M.I.T., Cornell, Rutgers, Purdue, Illinois, Minnesota,

Wisconsin, U.C. Berkeley and, here in Utah, Utah State University in Logan, founded in 1888.

Congress also used grants of public lands to subsidize the building of transportation infrastructure—wagon roads, canals, railroads, and highways—to knit newer states to the older ones.

There were, to be sure, disagreements over many of the details. But broadly speaking, Congress remained committed to carrying out the vision of the nation's founders, to use the public lands to foster orderly growth, prosperity, and most of all unity, as settlement expanded across the continent.

Then, as the nation's divide over slavery reached a fever pitch and civil war loomed, the U.S. Supreme Court unexpectedly created doubt about the breadth of Congress's power under the property clause of the Constitution. Its infamous decision in the *Dred Scott* case in 1857 is mostly known for Chief Justice Roger B. Taney's conclusion that African-Americans could never become citizens of the United States. But Taney also held that the property clause had no application outside the thirteen original states and thus gave Congress no power to address slavery in the territories or in admitting new states. The decision closed off the last remaining hope of ending slavery peacefully, through the political process, and helped plunge the nation into the Civil War.

This view of the property clause was unprecedented, without legal basis, and has never been followed. Indeed, the court's decision has been so discredited that Utah's hired lawyers do not rely on it, even though its states' rights slant on the property clause is the most favorable precedent available to them.

With the tragic slavery-related exception, the nation's public lands continued to play a crucial role in keeping the nation whole as it expanded to the Pacific, and they would soon come to play a role in healing the wounds of the Civil War.

A fourth myth is that the United States did not start retaining ownership of some public lands to serve national purposes until almost a century after the nation's founding.

Associated with the myths I've already mentioned, this one is put forward to try to show that the national government long held no expectation of ever holding onto ownership of any lands.

Again, the facts are to the contrary.[10] Almost from the beginning, Congress "reserved" some public lands for such national purposes as military bases, lighthouses, and Indian homelands. It also reserved public lands containing valuable minerals, salt springs, and forests so as to preserve public control of commodities vital to the nation and even, in 1832, set apart some public lands in Arkansas containing hot springs as a health resort.

During this same era, the U.S. also occasionally acquired lands from private owners for national purposes. In 1790, Congress authorized the purchase of land that formed part of the site of the U.S. Military Academy at West Point and, a few years later, thousands of acres of forested lands in the Southeast to supply timber for building naval vessels.

While these pre–Civil War public land reservations and acquisitions were not as large or as widespread as those made later, they illustrate how, practically from the nation's beginning, Congress grasped the wisdom of keeping some lands in public ownership to serve important national objectives.

Those objectives would naturally change over time as the nation expanded, its population grew, and its economy and culture evolved.

In the first few decades after the Civil War, a powerful political movement emerged that called for holding more and larger tracts of land in national ownership.

It had roots in that conflict, for just as it changed much else about America, the Civil War helped move public land policy in a new direction. It was no accident that the cohort of American politicians most directly involved in and deeply affected by that bloody struggle would lead the way—using the public lands to help, in Abraham Lincoln's timeless words, "bind up the nation's wounds."

It began modestly in 1864, when President Lincoln signed into law a measure passed by a war-weary Congress that required the

5. Yosemite by Carlton Watkins (Source: Library of Congress Prints and Photographs Division).

preservation of sizeable tracts of public land at a place in California called Yosemite for the sole purpose of making their inspirational qualities accessible to present and future generations. Sponsored by California Senator John Conness, an immigrant from Ireland, the legislation granted Yosemite Valley and a nearby grove of giant sequoia trees to the State of California (which had been admitted to the Union fourteen years before), on the strict condition, cemented into federal law, that they be protected forever in public ownership for general public enjoyment.

Because so few people had ever visited, most Americans were introduced to Yosemite's magnificence by Carleton Watkins's photographs. They had been displayed in a New York gallery immediately after an exhibit of the Matthew Brady Studio's shocking photographs of Civil War battlefield dead. This juxtaposition suggested, as historian Simon Schama put it in his book *Landscape and Memory*, that the Yosemite legislation was "a redemption for the national agony" wrought by the war. Protecting this iconic

6. Civil War dead by Alexander Gardner of Matthew Brady's studio (Source: Library of Congress Prints and Photographs Division).

American landscape in public hands for contemplation and inspiration helped put the nation on a path to mending.[11]

Eight years later, in 1872, Congress took another momentous step, protecting two million acres of public lands at a place called Yellowstone, a few hundred miles north of Utah. That legislation, signed into law by Civil War hero Ulysses S. Grant, moved a step beyond the Yosemite model, because it kept Yellowstone in permanent *national* ownership. It was the world's first national park.[12]

Yellowstone also illustrated the capacity of the public lands to mend the battle-torn nation. Not long after the park was established, developers came forward with schemes to carve it up, shrink its boundaries, and build a railroad through it. This triggered a political struggle that went on for well over a decade.

Two former enemies came together to lead the park's defense—General Philip Sheridan, Civil War hero and commander of the

7. Presidential party visiting Yellowstone in 1883: seated second from left, famed Civil War General Philip Sheridan; seated in center, President Chester A. Arthur; and seated at right, Missouri Senator (and former member of the Confederate Congress) George Vest (Source: Library of Congress Prints and Photographs Division).

Army of the West, and Missouri Senator George Vest, who had served in the Congress of the Confederacy throughout the Civil War. Sheridan and Vest persuaded President Chester A. Arthur, who in 1883 became the first sitting president to travel west and be inspired by the grandeur of the public lands, to come to the park's defense. Eventually, the U.S. Army was deployed to defend it from looters.[13]

A few years later, the connection between public lands and national healing was again on display. In September 1890, Congress began authorizing the purchase and preservation in U.S. ownership of the sites of Civil War battles like Gettysburg, Antietam, and Shiloh, and that same month created two large new national parks in California's Sierras—one encircling the valley of the Yosemite and another further south, at Sequoia.

Another key ingredient in this movement for preserving public lands was patriotic pride in preserving and showing off the nation's magnificent, mostly wild scenery, what historian Alfred Runte called "scenic nationalism."[14] Still another was the idea, popularized by the likes of Henry David Thoreau and John Muir, of the spiritual importance of connecting with the natural world.

Both of these might be said to reflect the Euro-Americans' absorption of the deep identification with and regard for their natural surroundings manifested by Native Americans.

Another factor was growing recognition—building on an influential book, *Man and Nature,* published in 1864 by a former Vermont Congressman, George Perkins Marsh—of the need to manage forested lands wisely in order to husband water and timber supplies, curb erosion, and temper destructive flooding. These matters were especially important in the rugged and arid American West.

As all this was brewing, there was a growing backlash across the country against industrial abuse of lands, both private and public, by logging, mining, and railroad interests. At the height of what Mark Twain called the Gilded Age, wealth was concentrated at the top and large corporations were subject to little regulation, mining was uncontrolled, and forests across the country were being plundered by what later came to be called "rape, ruin, and run" methods.[15]

The resulting environmental effects brought the wisdom of Marsh's teachings home to many Americans. Hydraulic mining in California's northern Sierra wreaked so much havoc upon downstream settlers and farmers that, in the 1880s, the courts enjoined the practice as a common law public nuisance. Flooding exacerbated by unchecked logging- and mining-related pollution wrought similar damage elsewhere.[16]

In the same era, large livestock grazing operations took over vast tracts of public lands without legal sanction. The result was, according to one landmark study, the conversion of millions of acres of grassland to desert,[17] as well as the erection of fences and the exclusion of potential settlers. Their practices brought to mind the demise of the English commons in an earlier era, a parallel underscored by the fact that a number of these grazing operations were owned by investors from the British Isles.[18]

8. "Copper King Senator" William Clark of Montana (Source: Library of Congress Prints and Photographs Division).

9. "Silver Senator" William Stewart of Nevada (Source: Library of Congress Prints and Photographs Division).

Two men whose fortunes derived from the public lands personified America's Gilded Age. One was William Stewart, the so-called "Silver Senator" from Nevada. Wallace Stegner called him a figure "to delight a caricaturist and depress a patriot." Wealthy from representing disputants in litigation over the famous Comstock Lode in Nevada, Stewart went to the U.S. Senate in late 1864 not yet forty but a millionaire, its richest member. Soon thereafter, he wrote and steered to enactment a law governing mining on public lands that was so complicated as to delight generations of lawyers. Stewart lived large, making and losing several fortunes in various ventures, most of them conducted while he was in public office. In 1873, he built a 19,000-square-foot mansion known as "Stewart's Castle" on Washington's DuPont Circle. Soon thereafter he left the Senate under a cloud after conspiring, for a share of the profits, to persuade some gullible Brits to invest in the failing Emma Mine in Utah's Little Cottonwood Canyon. After a twelve-year hiatus, the Nevada legislature returned him to the Senate in 1887, where he served until 1905. Stewart grudgingly accepted the idea that the national government might protect tracts of its land that contained what he called "novelties, curiosities, and strange developments of nature as places of resort." But reserving lands for broader purposes was, he warned his colleagues in 1897, "absurd," "folly," "barbarous," an "outrage upon the West," and, indeed, a "disgrace to American civilization."[19]

The second was William Clark, known as the "Copper King," one of the nation's wealthiest men. Mark Twain called him "as rotten a human being as can be found anywhere under the flag." As Montana prepared for statehood in 1889, Clark bribed his way into the presidency of the state's constitutional convention, where he told the delegates that the City of Butte's poor air quality, a product of his company's mining activities, did not pose an obstacle to its becoming the new state's capital. This was because, he said, "all the town's physicians consider the smoke" a "disinfectant," and ladies in particular were "very fond" of it because it had "just enough arsenic" to give them a "beautiful complexion." A few years later, after he bought one of Montana's seats in the U.S. Senate, he lectured his colleagues that Americans were "obliged to avail ourselves of all the [natural] resources at our command," and those who come after "can well take care of themselves."[20]

By the 1890s, though, the nation was turning sharply away from the Silver Senator's and the Copper King's messages of unrestrained greed with scant regard for others, including future generations, or for the environment. Scientific societies involved with forestry, archaeology, paleontology, ethnology, and similar disciplines were forming and advocating for keeping more lands in national ownership permanently for various purposes.

In 1891, Congress approved what came to be known as the Forest Reserve Act, which some consider the single most consequential piece of public lands legislation ever enacted. It expanded a long-standing congressional practice of delegating authority to the executive branch to hold onto public lands for various purposes by vesting the president with sweeping power to reserve vast tracts of public lands in permanent U.S. ownership to protect their value as watersheds.

It culminated more than a decade of strenuous efforts, inside Congress and across the nation, to keep much of the nation's remaining public lands not suitable for conventional farming from falling into the hands of large corporations. It resulted in dozens of forest reserves that eventually became a system of national forests that embraced nearly two hundred million acres, or about 8 percent of the nation's lands.

By the last decade of the nineteenth century other new voices were becoming influential. Public interest in protecting wildlife and its habitat was growing, largely in reaction to the rapid destruction of American bison, the passenger pigeon, and millions of colorful birds plundered for fashion. The effort was led by sport hunters and by growing numbers of politically engaged women who were, particularly in the western U.S., beginning to gain the right to vote. In Congress, the effort was spearheaded by Civil War veteran John F. Lacey of Iowa.

Not long after armed conflicts between Indians and the United States came to an end, Native Americans and their rich cultures began to be appreciated rather than feared. As this happened, interest grew in protecting cultural and archaeological resources found on many public lands. It led to the landmark Antiquities Act of 1906, about which much has been heard lately. Shepherded through Congress by John Lacey, it extended the congressional practice of giving the executive broad authority by authorizing the president to preserve public lands containing features of "historic or scientific interest" as national monuments.

The powerful movement to protect significant amounts of land in U.S. ownership that was woven from all these strands—patriotism, scenic nationalism, science, a backlash against the Gilded Age, growing interest in conserving wildlife and cultural resources—played out in ways that explode two more myths about the public lands.

One is that the movement was confined to western states. The other is that the effort was limited to lands the U.S. already owned.

In both cases, the opposite is true.

Starting around the turn of the twentieth century, the movement found fertile ground across the entire nation. President Theodore Roosevelt established forest reserves on public lands in Arkansas, Florida, Kansas, Oklahoma, and Puerto Rico. Beginning in 1903, he established bird reservations on public lands in Florida, Louisiana, and Michigan, as well as in the West, and almost immediately Congress chimed in with support. Their combined efforts eventually produced a large national system of wildlife refuges.

The Antiquities Act of 1906 broke new ground by authorizing the U.S. to accept donations of land to protect them permanently. This opened the door for private philanthropists to make significant additions to the nation's bounty of protected places. Muir Woods in California and what eventually became Acadia National Park in Maine were the earliest examples, in 1908 and 1916, respectively. Many more, as at Wyoming's Jackson Hole, followed.

In 1911, Congress launched a major new program to establish forest reserves in the East, South, and Midwest. Its primary sponsor was Congressman John Weeks of Massachusetts, who convinced the powerful Speaker of the House, Joseph Cannon—a man who had earlier scorned the idea, allegedly with the quip "not one cent for scenery"—to let the legislation proceed through the Congress.[21]

The Weeks Act was a counterpart to the forest reserve legislation Congress had enacted twenty years earlier, but it differed in two important ways. For one thing, rather than simply reserving lands the U.S. already owned, it authorized the acquisition of private lands into national ownership. Second, because a good deal of that land had already been logged, it was the first major land restoration program in American history.

Over the next few decades, the Weeks Act resulted in the establishment of many new national forests, encompassing some twenty-five million acres in more than two dozen states in the East, South, and Midwest. In that same era, Congress authorized the acquisition of millions of acres in national parks and wildlife preserves across the nation.

This brings me to yet another myth about the public lands; namely, that they were safeguarded mostly over the opposition of local residents and state governments.

This myth finds especially fertile ground out here in the West. It makes for a nice story line—the ruggedly independent West would, of course, fiercely oppose decisions by the national government to keep large tracts of western lands in national ownership and control.

There's just one problem with it. It's mostly untrue.

For one thing, the American West in the decades leading up to the twentieth century was hardly as ruggedly independent as myth would have it. Far more westerners died in industrial mining and railroad accidents than in gunfights or Indian wars.[22] By the 1890s, the West had a larger percentage of its population living in urban areas than any other region in the nation. Its growing cities and land developers were asking that the uplands that supplied them with water be protected. So were rural settlers, who wanted to safeguard water supplies for crop irrigation, a necessity in much of the arid region. Moreover, by 1891, the continental West was almost fully represented in the Congress, with only Utah, Arizona, and New Mexico still in territorial status.

There were occasional grumbles that the national government did not always make wise decisions in drawing boundaries around the lands it was reserving, or consult enough with the locals. Some things never change.

But the facts are beyond dispute and speak loudly: far from being the result of a distant national government overpowering local opposition, these reservations mostly had the enthusiastic support of people in the affected region. Indeed, practically all the national parks, most of the forest reserves, and many of the national monuments came about as a result of petitions to the national government submitted by states and local residents and their political representatives.[23]

Several examples illustrate the point. The first forest reserve in Utah was established in the Wasatch Mountains by President Grover

10. President Grover Cleveland (Source: U.S. National Archives and Records Administration).

11. Utah Governor Heber Wells, Republican (Source: Utah State Historical Society, used by permission).

Cleveland in 1897, the year after Utah became a state. Cleveland had the strong support of Utah's first governor, Heber Wells, who greased the skids for the president's action by withdrawing from sale and settlement state-owned lands inside the proposed federal reserve.

In the years that followed, other leading Utah politicians played similarly prominent roles in public land reservations, leading one historian to note that the national parks and forests established in the state had the "hearty approval of most Utahns."[24] Senator Reed Smoot, who represented Utah in the U.S. Senate from 1903 to 1933, was an active supporter of Theodore Roosevelt's vigorous public lands conservation initiatives, backed John Muir's campaign to stop the Hetch Hetchy Dam project in Yosemite National Park, and was a primary sponsor of legislation that established several new national parks and the National Park Service itself.

This history lends considerable irony to the fact that Utah today is the principal locus of the movement to reduce protections for, and to divest the U.S. of control of many public lands.[25]

12. Utah Senator Reed Smoot, Republican (Source: Library of Congress Prints and Photographs Division).

Grassroots support for public land reservations can also be measured at the ballot box. Theodore Roosevelt was more responsible for the public lands we see today than any other single individual in American history. He tripled the size of the national forest system, launched what became a nation-wide system of wildlife refuges, and used the Antiquities Act eighteen times to protect more than 1.5 million acres.

He could not and would not have done all this without grass-roots support. In 1904, when Roosevelt's campaign to expand protected public lands was already well underway, he carried every western state in the presidential election, including every county in Colorado where forest reserves had been created except one, which he lost by a scant twenty-five votes. This was a considerable improvement over his predecessor, William McKinley, who in 1900 had failed to carry Nevada, Idaho, Montana, and Colorado, and all but one of those rural Colorado counties.[26]

At the instigation of a handful of western senators, Congress eventually did take a few steps to curb Roosevelt's authority, most notably when, in 1907, it limited his power to create new forest reserves in six western states. Conspicuously, Utah was not among the six.

Roosevelt was not deterred, using his remaining time in office to protect more and more public land. In the meantime, Congress itself made new reservations, authorized acquisitions of other lands, and never made any serious effort to undo Roosevelt's actions.[27]

The movement's grassroots popularity is also reflected in the Weeks Act of 1911. It required states to consent to the U.S. acquisition of land within their borders. A number of states were so enthusiastic they enacted the necessary authorization even before the act emerged from Congress. Illustrating once again how public lands provided a common ground to unite different interests, Democratic governors from the South joined Republican governors from the North in support of the bill. Massachusetts Governor Curtis Guild suggested that it was the first time representatives from the southern and the New England states had ever appeared jointly before the Congress "to ask for something for the common welfare of the United States."[28]

In the next quarter century, state governments purchased many private lands and then donated them to the national government for their protection. Indeed, the statutory template Congress used to establish major national parks in the East, Midwest, and South—at Shenandoah, Virginia (1925); Mammoth Cave, Kentucky (1925); Great Smoky Mountains, North Carolina and Tennessee (1926); Isle Royale, Michigan (1931); Everglades, Florida (1934); and Big Bend, Texas (1935)—required that the lands involved "be secured by the United States only by public or private donation."[29]

One more myth has taken root; namely, that holding onto and protecting public lands has been inextricably bound up in partisan politics.

In recent years, protection of public lands is much more identified with the Democratic than the Republican Party. I will come back to that shortly. But for nearly all of the nation's history, the protection movement has been fundamentally bipartisan, with the proponents' party allegiance never playing a significant role.

Here are a few examples: The key congressional architects of the 1891 legislation that led to the national forest system were Republican Congressman Lewis Payson of Illinois and Democratic Congressman William Holman of Indiana. Presidents Benjamin Harrison and William McKinley, both Republicans, and Grover Cleveland, a Democrat, each vigorously exercised the authority, together establishing nearly fifty million acres of forest reserves.

Indeed, the Republican legacy is especially prominent. John Lacey, John Weeks, and Utah's Governor Wells and Senator Smoot were, like Theodore Roosevelt, Republicans. In the 1920s and early 1930s, Republican Presidents Harding, Coolidge, and Hoover used the Antiquities Act to protect millions of acres of public lands in places like Utah's Bryce Canyon (Harding), Glacier Bay, Alaska (Coolidge), and California's Death Valley and Colorado's Black Canyon of the Gunnison (Hoover). Coolidge and Hoover also set in motion the campaign to create new national parks in the eastern part of the nation. Republican President Eisenhower used the Antiquities Act to protect the C&O Canal in Washington DC, today the most popular recreational area in the capital region, two days before John F. Kennedy was inaugurated.[30]

How the last big chunk of public lands in the lower-forty-eight states was reserved from divestiture in the 1930s drives home the truth about grassroots and bipartisan support. Because it included a good deal of land in Utah, the episode is worth examining.

In 1929 President Hoover called for a systematic examination of the nation's remaining so-called "public domain," the term commonly applied to those mostly arid public lands located primarily in the interior West that had not already been reserved in forests, parks, or other protected status. He suggested that the U.S. should retain parts of this remaining public domain that had a "distinctly national as well as local importance," but offered to transfer other lands chiefly valuable for livestock grazing to the states.

Republican Representative Don Colton of Utah sponsored the resolution that created a committee to study Hoover's suggestion, which came to be known as the Garfield Committee after its chair, former Interior Secretary James R. Garfield. On the House floor, Colton explained that the lack of "supervision or control" on these nearly two hundred million acres of arid public lands had led to

13. Congressman Don Colton of Utah, Republican (Source: Harris and Ewing Collection at the Library of Congress).

overgrazing and severe erosion, with the lands "being ruined," calling into question "the future of the livestock industry in the West."

Most of the Committee's nineteen members were from the Intermountain West, and its 1931 report basically endorsed Hoover's suggestion. It recommended that the U.S. reserve additional lands that were important for forest, park, monument, and wildlife refuge purposes. Leftover public domain thought valuable "chiefly for the production of forage" should be offered to the states, but "impressed with a trust" that required the lands' "rehabilitation" and included such other "restrictions as Congress might deem appropriate." States would have ten years to decide whether to accept the offer, and if they declined, the committee called for the lands to be retained by the U.S. and managed in a fashion similar to the national forests.

The Garfield Committee proposed that the U.S. retain the mineral rights in any land transferred to states, but, as President Hoover had noted to the western governors in suggesting the transfer idea in the first place, federal retention of mineral rights did not seriously impair state interests. This was because, by the terms of the Mineral Leasing Act adopted in 1920, Congress was already effectively giving 90 percent of the mineral revenues it derived from these lands to the states.[31]

The western states, led by Utah's Governor George Dern, spurned the Garfield Committee's recommendation, and so Congress never seriously considered it. In the words of Louise Peffer, the episode's

14. Congressman Edward Taylor of Colorado, Democrat (Source: Harris and Ewing Collection at the Library of Congress).

leading historian, its quick political death "clarified opinion" in support of continuing national ownership, in effect giving Congress an "all-clear signal" to enact legislation that would, for the first time, control livestock grazing on these lands to rehabilitate them and safeguard their public values.

Utah Representative Colton promptly introduced a bill to take steps to restore these lands to health. It passed the House in 1932 but got no further before he lost in the Democratic tidal wave in that fall's elections. At that point, Democratic Congressman Edward Taylor from western Colorado, who had grown up in a cattle-raising family in northwestern Kansas, pushed the idea to enactment.

For much of Taylor's long career in the Colorado legislature and then the Congress, he had considered the policy of keeping public rangelands out of private hands "un-American." But he changed his mind because, as he later put it, he saw "waste, competition, overuse, and abuse of valuable range lands and watersheds" that threatened the "basic economy of entire communities." Only the U.S. government, he concluded, could "cope with the situation," because the job was "too big" for "even the states to handle." Once convinced, he pursued reform with, in Louise Peffer's words, "the zeal of a convert."

The Taylor Grazing Act became law in 1934. Final passage in the House was by a nearly three-to-one margin; the Senate passed it on a voice vote after Colorado Senator Alva Adams summed up western sentiment this way on the Senate floor: "None of us like[s] to be regulated, and that is probably more true in western areas than anywhere else," but regulation "is preferable to overgrazing and lack of regulation" that currently prevails on these lands.

The act quickly led to a combination of executive and further congressional action that kept about 150 million acres, most of the remaining unreserved arid lands of the Intermountain West and Southwest—including about 40 percent of Utah—in national ownership.[32]

This effectively ended large-scale divestitures of public lands, outside the special case of Alaska. At around the same time, the U.S. embarked on a parallel restoration program that involved re-acquiring into national ownership failed Dust Bowl homesteads. This created a system of national grasslands across a dozen states in the western half of the nation.

Over the decades that followed, the Garfield Committee's recommendation to put deserving areas of the remaining arid public lands in national parks, monuments, refuges, and other protected status was gradually implemented. As appreciation of the marvelous scenic, archaeological, cultural, biological, and other values of these lands steadily grew, Congress and the executive protected millions of acres at places like Capitol Reef, Canyonlands, Great Basin, and Joshua Tree National Parks, Organ Pipe Cactus National Monument, and Mohave National Preserve, and added millions more acres to reserves established earlier at places like Dinosaur National Monument, Grand Canyon, Grand Teton, Zion, Bryce Canyon, Saguaro, Death Valley, Great Sand Dunes, Wupatki, Craters of the Moon, Petrified Forest, and Black Canyon of the Gunnison.

Congress and the executive have also protected millions of acres of public lands as wilderness or wilderness study or roadless areas or through other means. The period from 1964 to 1980 was particularly fruitful, for it produced such landmark public land laws as the Wilderness Act, an organic act for the National Wildlife Refuge system, the Federal Land Policy and Management Act, significant reforms of the national forest and national park organic acts, and, topping it off, the clumsily titled Alaska National Interest Lands

Conservation Act, or ANILCA. Enacted in 1980, it put more than one hundred million acres of public land in Alaska in national parks, wildlife refuges, and other protected statuses.[33]

Now let me circle back toward the first myth I mentioned—that the public lands have been a divisive force in American national life—and offer one more; namely, that for the last century and a quarter, the American people have blown hot and cold on the wisdom of protecting public lands in national ownership.

To be sure, America has always had a minority of citizens who basically subscribe to libertarian principles, who dislike the idea of the government owning and managing a lot of land, and indeed, who are critical of government almost regardless of what it does. This portion of the electorate has waxed and waned somewhat over time, influenced by things like the general health of the economy.

But the historical record is clear that for more than a century, a large majority of Americans, inside as well as outside the West, have strongly supported the national government holding large amounts of land in common ownership for common purpose. That policy has not, in other words, been a source of genuinely deep division in the nation's politics and culture.

The consistent results of public opinion polls taken over the last several years make clear that—despite some strident critics—this remains true today. As Gifford Pinchot, Theodore Roosevelt's close ally and the first chief of the U.S. Forest Service, observed in describing the establishment of the early forest reserves, as is "usual in public matters, those who were for made far less noise than those who were against."[34]

So, finally, what lessons can we draw about America's public lands from a clear-eyed look at their history?

It seems to me hard to quarrel with the idea that America's preservation of large amounts of land in national ownership has been extraordinarily visionary. Open to all, protecting our outdoor heritage, our wildlife, and many important chapters in the American story, providing inspiration, education, and recreation to people from all walks of life, across the nation and indeed the world, they are a priceless legacy to hand down to succeeding generations, perhaps the best example of governmental thinking for the long term that I know.[35]

In his 1971 environmental message, President Richard Nixon called the public lands the "'breathing space' of the Nation."[36] Evidence has steadily emerged to support the idea that the public lands are good for mental as well as physical health.

More than 80 percent of Americans now live in urban areas, a percentage that has doubled since 1900. Over that time, the West has remained the nation's most urbanized region; today, more than 90 percent of westerners live in urban areas. Yet humans evolved in a biocentric world. Modern science is providing more and more confirmation of what the likes of Aristotle and Wordsworth and Darwin and Muir knew—that our brains respond favorably to encounters with the natural world.

Numerous studies show that people are significantly happier outdoors in natural habitats than they are in urban environments. Forest walkers have lower stress than urban walkers. Recovery time of hospital patients is significantly shortened if their rooms have windows looking out on greenery. A spate of popular books make this point, with titles like *The Nature Fix* drawing attention to conditions like "nature-deficit disorder."

America's public lands have also offered valuable lessons to other nations. For well over a century, our policies have been emulated around the world, starting with the national parks, sometimes called the "best idea we ever had."[37]

The U.S. has also been a pioneer in using public lands to protect wildlife habitat on a large scale. With a sizable portion of the world's species now threatened with extinction, the eminent biologist E. O. Wilson recently advocated setting aside about half our planet's surface as a protected natural reserve.[38] In the U.S., our protected public lands are a large step in that direction.[39]

These public lands are also good for the economy, local and regional as well as national. They are magnets for travel and tourism. The outdoor recreation industry—closely linked to the public lands—is becoming one of the nation's largest and most job-intensive economic sectors.

Public lands also enhance quality of life in nearby communities and help attract retiring Baby Boomers who have significant nonlabor income, and businesses who tout access to them as a talent-recruiting and retention tool. Studies of counties all across the West consistently show a direct correlation between their economic prosperity and the percentage of protected public lands within their borders.[40]

The public lands can also be seen as a great bargain—by practically every measure one of the most cost-effective things the U.S. government does. The total annual budget of the four principal government agencies that manage these six hundred-plus million acres is in the neighborhood of $13 billion. That figure does not reflect the offsetting billions of dollars that oil and gas and other resources extracted from the public lands produce for the Treasury every year. Moreover, that money is spent on many things besides stewardship, visitor services, and science, especially to fight wildfires, a responsibility the nation assumes mainly to protect structures on nearby private lands.

That $13 billion is a mere 2 percent of the nearly $600 billion the U.S. spends per year in the nondefense, discretionary (nonentitlement) portion of the federal budget. It's less than one-third of one per cent of the total $3.8 trillion federal budget. Furthermore, the four federal land management agencies collectively employ only about 3 percent of the U.S. government's total civilian workforce (not counting the U.S. Postal Service).

Still, while there is much to celebrate and treasure about America's public lands, let me close with a warning.

Some libertarians call the public lands "political lands." They use the term rather scornfully, but they are exactly right. The public

U.S. GOVERNMENT ANNUAL BUDGET BY CATEGORY

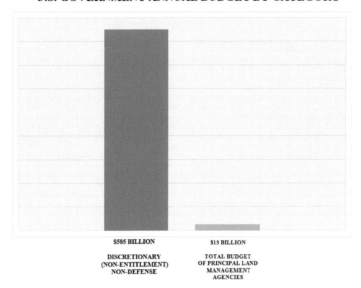

$585 BILLION

DISCRETIONARY
(NON-ENTITLEMENT)
NON-DEFENSE

$13 BILLION

TOTAL BUDGET
OF PRINCIPAL LAND
MANAGEMENT
AGENCIES

15. Relative proportion of budget of federal land management agencies versus overall government discretionary (nonentitlement) nondefense budget and employment (Source: John Leshy and Lesley King).

CIVILIAN WORK FORCE OF U.S. GOVERNMENT
(excluding USPS)

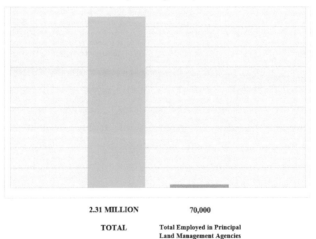

2.31 MILLION

TOTAL

70,000

Total Employed in Principal
Land Management Agencies

16. Relative proportion of work force of federal land management agencies versus total civilian workforce of U.S. government (Source: John Leshy and Lesley King).

lands remain a creature of politics and our political system. This means their future is hardly guaranteed.

While the national government has, as I have described, so far generally safeguarded public lands for future generations, they can be eliminated. Let's not kid ourselves. Ownership can be transferred to the states or the private sector. No public land—not even iconic treasures like Yellowstone or Zion—is immune. All it takes is simple, ordinary legislation. Congress could do it tomorrow.

Moreover, even if Congress does not act, existing law gives the executive branch considerable authority to transfer effective control over many of these lands to states or the private sector, through leases and other long-term legal arrangements.

What it boils down to is this: each new generation of Americans must effectively decide what it wants to do with these lands. Without political support, public lands and the values they bring to us can be lost.

Now, do friends of the public lands have genuine cause for concern?

On the one hand, as I mentioned, just about every public opinion poll conducted just about everywhere shows continuing strong popular support for protecting the public lands.

But there are good reasons not to be complacent. We seem to be struggling over the principles on which our country was founded, and our political culture is increasingly polarized. Related to this, our political system is swamped with money and its pursuit occupies much of the time and energy of politicians at all levels. Moreover, a relentless campaign funded by deep-pocketed interests has succeeded in undermining trust in government and science in the eyes of a significant portion of Americans.[41] The results are plain to see. A seemingly growing number of Americans vilify the national government and politics, find it easy to disregard the teachings of science, and regard collective action, even of the most justifiable kind, as a threat to individual liberty.

All this makes public lands—a prominent symbol of government, particularly in the West—a target.

One result has been the withdrawal of Republican Party support for holding and protecting public lands. In a stark departure from its long history of championing public land conservation, beginning in the 1990s the party began officially endorsing a program to divest some public lands to the states or private sector.[42] In 2016, one plank in its platform called on Congress to "immediately pass universal legislation providing for a timely and orderly mechanism requiring the federal government to convey certain federally controlled public lands to states," and called upon "all national and state leaders and representatives to exert their utmost power and influence to urge the transfer of those lands."[43]

So far, the idea of outright transfer of significant amounts of land has not gained political traction. But a number of our leaders in Washington are currently working to shift as much control over public lands as possible to state and local governments and the private sector. It is telling that this is happening at the same time some wealthy owners of large tracts of private lands are closing traditional access not only to their lands, but to adjacent public lands as well.[44]

These trends have led some to suggest that America is in a new Gilded Age,[45] where comparisons might be drawn between our current president and his interior secretary and figures like Senators Stewart and Clark.

Another storm cloud is that the administration and its allies in the Congress have proposed severe cuts in federal land management agency budgets. President Trump's proposed 2018 budget would have reduced funds for the Park Service by 13 percent, which would have been the largest single-year reduction since the end of the Second World War. His 2019 budget would have cut the Park Service by 7 percent and the Interior Department overall by 16 percent.

Such reductions could not come at a worse time. Recreational visits to public lands are skyrocketing. The National Park System set attendance records in 2014, 2015, and 2016. In 1980, there were slightly more than two million visitors to Grand Canyon; in 2011, more than four million; last year, more than six million. Similar

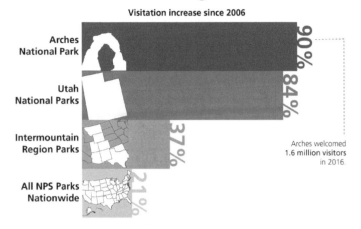

How did we get here?

Visitation increase since 2006

Arches
National Park — 90%

Utah
National Parks — 84%

Intermountain
Region Parks — 37%

All NPS Parks
Nationwide — 21%

Arches welcomed
1.6 million visitors
in 2016.

17. Growth in visitation to national parks, 2006–2016 (Source: National Park Service, Chris Wonderly).

trends are found on public lands here in Utah and all around the country.[46]

Challenges posed by climate change make the jobs of these agencies even more difficult. A big increase in the number and intensity of wildfires is only the most visible indicator, and fighting these fires is a major drain on agency resources.[47]

Slashing agency budgets when public lands are being overwhelmed by visitors and other challenges would inevitably make it harder for those agencies to fulfill their stewardship mission of protecting these lands while keeping them accessible for public use. Closing field offices and shrinking agency workforces distance the agencies from the general public. Over time this will inevitably sap public confidence in federal management and, with it, public support for the public lands.

Such a downward spiral seems to be exactly what many advocates of such budget cutting intend, to cause government to falter and lose the confidence of the public.

Finally, it is a reason for concern that we all, especially younger Americans, may grow too addicted to the attractions our gadgets offer us to pay much attention to, or learn to cherish, the marvelous resources found on the public lands.

No one could argue that all public land management policies and decisions have been wise. Our democratic system is, after all, controlled by humans, who can act with stupidity and shortsightedness as well as with intelligence and vision. No reasonable person would argue that every acre of public land should remain in national ownership, or that the U.S. should never acquire another acre, or that public land policies cannot be improved. Some land ownership patterns could be reconfigured to allow for more coherent management. Some public land decision-making processes could be made simpler or otherwise reformed to better serve the public interest.

But today's sour, polarized, cynical political climate makes it practically impossible to make progress even on measures that command wide public support.

One way to begin to change the political culture and reduce the polarization is to rekindle appreciation of the unifying role the public lands have played over the long sweep of the nation's history and to celebrate the bipartisan workings of our political system that have produced the results we see today. We should revere the inspired actions of many people, some known and many unknown, who have helped safeguard this vast public asset—our common ground, as it were—allowing it to nurture national pride, physical and mental health, and a spirit of community in an increasingly diverse nation.

It is, in other words, particularly important and timely to remind ourselves that America's public lands are a huge political success story and a credit to the workings of our political system and our government, particularly our national government.

Only time will tell whether current efforts to divest the U.S. of ownership or control of the public lands will succeed, or whether Americans will continue to embrace their public lands.

I hope the embrace will continue, and that more people will pay heed to something that John Muir wrote as the nineteenth century was drawing to a close:

"People are beginning to find out that going to the mountains is going home, that wildness is a necessity, and that parks and reservations are useful not only as fountains of timber and irrigating rivers, but as fountains of life."[48]

Notes

1. See Leshy, "Are the U.S. Public Lands Unconstitutional?", *Hastings Law Journal* 69, no. 2 (2018):499, 503.
2. They do not include military lands, submerged lands offshore, or lands held by the United States in trust for Indians.
3. I don't want to leave the impression that all or even most of the U.S. public lands have remained in substantially natural condition. Some of these lands have been subject to conventional economic development. Mining has taken place on some public lands since the California Gold Rush. Over much of the twentieth century, numerous dams and reservoirs and other waterworks have been constructed on some of them. Trees on public lands have been harvested and forests burned by human activities over centuries. Forests on what is now public land in the East saw significant harvests for many decades, and many forests in the Northwest saw major logging starting with the post–World War II building boom through the late 1980s. Livestock grazing has long been found on more than two hundred million acres of public lands and continues on many of these lands today. In recent years numerous solar and wind generation plants have been located on public lands. Despite all this activity, it bears repeating that the vast majority of public land acreage remains unroaded and appears mostly natural. Appearances of course can be deceiving. More is steadily being learned about how Native Americans impacted the landscape, even in places like Yosemite, and about how the European invaders who came after changed what look to the untutored eye like natural landscapes even more, and not always for the better. A seminal work here is William Cronon, *Changes in the Land: Indians, Colonists, and the Ecology of New England* (New York: Hill and Wang, 1983). Still, with the exception of grazing by domestic livestock, the vast majority of public lands are today not being used for conventional resource extraction or industrial development.
4. Much of the history in this essay is drawn from Leshy, *supra* note 1, at 504–12, 517–31, 541–59, 572–80 and sources cited there.

5. For a detailed examination of Utah's claim, see Leshy, *supra* note 1. Utah Senator Mike Lee recently set forth arguments for the state taking over public lands in a speech to the Sutherland Institute, "Honoring the Founders' Promise on Federal Lands" (June 19, 2018), https://www.lee. senate.gov/public/index.cfm/2018/6honoring-the-founders-promise-on-federal-lands.

6. Richard B. Morris, "The Forging of the Union Reconsidered: A Historical Refutation of State Sovereignty over Seabeds," *Columbia Law Review* 74, no. 6 (1974):1056, 1057, 1089.

7. Considerable detail on this is provided in Leshy, *supra* note 1, at 521–27.

8. Texas was the prominent exception here, having already established its independence from Mexico when it was admitted to the Union. See Leshy, *supra* note 1, at 517–18.

9. This requirement had first been formulated by the founding generation as part of the famous Northwest Ordinance of 1787. See Leshy, *supra* note 1, at 509. It was repeatedly endorsed by the U.S. Congress in admitting new states.

10. The history is briefly summarized in Leshy, *supra* note 1, at 518–19. For example, several hundred thousand acres of public forested lands were reserved, and some were purchased from private owners, in both the original thirteen and newer states. See, e.g., Jenks Cameron, *The Development of Governmental Forest Control in the United States* (Baltimore: Johns Hopkins University Press, 1928), 28–71.

11. Simon Schama, *Landscape and Memory* (New York: Knopf, 1995), 7. California did such a lousy job of managing the Yosemite Grant that, in 1905, it ceded ownership back to the U.S. See 34 Stat. 831 (1905); John Ise, *Our National Park Policy: A Critical History* (Baltimore: Johns Hopkins University Press for Resources for the Future, 1961), 69–70.

12. See generally Richard A. Bartlett, *Yellowstone: A Wilderness Besieged* (Tucson: University of Arizona Press, 1985).

13. Sheridan's prominent role in subjugating Plains Indians as commander of the Army in the West made him controversial but, according to a leading historical study, he "mellowed over the years," expressing second thoughts about the harshness of his tactics, which suggests that his vigorous defense of Yellowstone and the region's wildlife was perhaps in part a kind of penance. See generally George Black, *Empire of Shadows* (New York: St. Martin's Press, 2012), especially at pp. 424–25. For a discussion of the military role at Yellowstone, see H. Duane Hampton, *How the U.S. Cavalry Saved Our National Parks* (Bloomington: Indiana University Press, 1971).

14. Alfred Runte, *National Parks: The American Experience* (Lincoln: University of Nebraska Press, 1979), 71.

15. This colorful phrase was, so far as I have been able to determine, coined by my former boss, the late Interior Secretary Cecil Andrus, who was a logger in his youth. See *Detroit Free Press*, December 3, 1979.

16. See, e.g., Leshy, *The Mining Law: A Study in Perpetual Motion* (Resources for the Future, 1987), 184–86, 440–41.

17. See, e.g., Philip Foss, *Politics and Grass: The Administration of Grazing on the Public Domain* (Seattle: University of Washington Press, 1960), 4. See also Donald Worster, *Under Western Skies: Nature and History in the American West* (New York: Oxford University Press, 1992), 45.

18. See, e.g., Christopher Knowlton, *Cattle Kingdom: The Hidden History of the Cowboy West* (Boston: Houghton Mifflin Harcourt, 2017), 96–97.

19. Stewart was chosen by the Nevada legislature to be one of the new state's first senators. Mark Twain, thanks to the influence of his brother Orion, briefly served on Senator Stewart's staff in this era, memorializing the experience (though without identifying Stewart by name) in 1868 in a satire of members of Congress that is still funny today. "My Late Senatorial Secretaryship," *The Galaxy*, May 1868, http://www.twainquotes.com/Galaxy/186805.html. Twain's biographer Justin Kaplan described the tall, bearded, long-haired Stewart as looking like an "archetypal frontier senator" and being "possessed by augustitude" in Kaplan, *Mr. Clemens and Mark Twain* (New York: Simon and Schuster, 1966), 58. Over his long political career, Stewart's chief loyalty was to himself. He first identified with the Whigs, then the Democrats, then became a Republican at the onset of the Civil War, then a Silver Republican who endorsed the Democrat William Jennings Bryan for president in 1896, and then once again a Republican. Background on Stewart and the Emma Mine can be found in Dan Plazak, *A Hole in the Ground with a Liar at the Top* (Salt Lake City: University of Utah Press, 2006), 59–77; and W. Turrentine Jackson, "The Infamous Emma Mine: A British Interest in the Little Cottonwood District, Utah Territory," *Utah History Quarterly* 23 (1955):339–62. His Senate speech attacking forest reserves is found at 32 Cong. Rec. 1280–81 (May 27, 1897).

20. See Duane A. Smith, *Mining America: The Industry and the Environment, 1800–1980* (Lawrence: University Press of Kansas, 1987), 45, 82; Michael P. Malone, "Midas of the West: The Incredible Career of William Andrews Clark," *Montana Magazine* (Autumn 1983):14. Malone called Clark "an especially virulent example of the unrestrained capitalist on the frontier." (Malone, 2). Fittingly, Clark bought Stewart's DuPont Circle mansion in preparing to move to Washington, but he never occupied it.

21. Gifford Pinchot, *Breaking New Ground* (Washington, DC: Island Press, 1987; repr. of New York: Harcourt, Brace, 1947), 240.

22. Euro-American settlement was never characterized by individuals going off into the wilds. Instead there was, as historian Garry Wills has noted, a "massive social effort" to bring order to western settlements. Garry Wills, *A Necessary Evil* (New York: Simon and Schuster, 1999), 249–51. Political movements to give women the right to vote, to prohibit the sale of alcoholic beverages, and to control guns were all prominent in the West during this period. As Wills put it, the "myth of frontier individualism—of

the man whose gun made him his own master, free and untrammeled—
dies hard. . . . But the gun did not tame the West. The West had to tame the
gun." (Wills, 251). See also W. Eugene Hollon, *Frontier Violence: Another
Look* (New York: Oxford University Press, 1974); Richard Slotkin,
Gunfighter Nation: The Myth of the Frontier in Twentieth Century America
(Norman: University of Oklahoma Press, 1972).

23. Interior Secretary Ryan Zinke perpetuated this myth in his report to
President Trump on national monuments. The fifth sentence of his
twenty-page report claimed that the very first use of the Antiquities Act,
President Theodore Roosevelt's establishment of Devil's Tower National
Monument in Wyoming a few weeks after the law was enacted, was
controversial. (https://www.doi.gov/sites/doi.gov/files/uploads/revised_
final_report.pdf). This was not true, as a few clicks on the internet would
have shown. Roosevelt acted at the invitation of Wyoming Congressman
Frank Mondell. Some years earlier Wyoming Senator Francis Warren had
promoted the Tower's inclusion in a forest reserve and introduced
legislation in Congress to make it a national park. Roosevelt's use of the
Antiquities Act to protect Devil's Tower encountered no opposition.
https://www.nps.gov/deto/learn/historyculture/first-fifty-years-
monument-established.htm.

24. Thomas G. Alexander, "Senator Reed Smoot and Western Land Policy,
1905–1920," *Arizona & the West* 13 (1970):245, 247–53.

25. One of Utah's arguments—that it was promised title to all the public lands
when it was admitted to the Union—is demonstrably false. See Leshy,
supra note 1, at 553–57. Another—that the state has been victimized by the
presence of so many public lands within its borders—is belied by the fact
that Utah's Department of Tourism has long campaigned to have people
visit its "Mighty 5" national parks, noting with pride that these public lands
"draw several million visitors from around the world each year to marvel at
surreal scenery and [engage in] unforgettable activities." https://www.
visitutah.com/places-to-go/most-visited-parks/the-mighty-5/

26. On the 1904 election results in Colorado counties, see G. Michael
McCarthy, *Hour of Trial: The Conservation Conflict in Colorado and the
West, 1891–1907* (Norman: University of Oklahoma Press, 1977), 293n107.
The presidential election results by state are easily accessible on Wikipedia.

27. In 1908, Roosevelt's anointed successor, W. H. Taft, did almost as well at the
ballot box in the West, losing only Colorado and Nevada, and those mostly
because Taft's opponent, William Jennings Bryan, supported the unlimited
coinage of silver. That issue attracted miners and some farmers, but had
almost nothing to do with reservations of public lands. In 1912, after a
campaign in which no candidate seriously challenged Roosevelt's public
land legacy, Democrat Woodrow Wilson carried eight of the eleven
western states.

28. Hearings before the Committee on Agriculture on what became the Weeks
Act, 60th Cong. 2d sess. (1909); see generally https://foresthistory.org/

research-explore/us-forest-service-history/policy-and-law/the-weeks-act/
passing-weeks-act/.

29. See, e.g., 46 Stat. 1514 (1931) (Isle Royale).

30. See, e.g., D. Harmon, F. P. McManamon and D. T. Pitcaithley, eds., *The Antiquities Act* ((Tucson: University of Arizona Press, 2006).

31. In his August 21, 1929 message to the western governors, President Hoover wrote: "Inasmuch as the royalties from mineral rights revert to the western states either direct or through the Reclamation Fund, their reservation to the federal control is not of the nature of a deprival." http://www.presidency.ucsb.edu/ws/index.php?pid=21899&st=&st1=

32. Louise Peffer, *The Closing of the Public Domain* (Stanford: Stanford University Press, 1951), 203–24.

33. Many of the public lands are, of course, further protected by a spate of laws, enacted mostly in the 1960s and 1970s, including the Wilderness Act, which prohibits roads and most commercial activities, and the Wild and Scenic Rivers Act. The Endangered Species Act that dates from the same era has provided further legal protection for such key public land habitats as old growth forests in the Northwest inhabited by creatures like the endangered northern spotted owl, spawning grounds for endangered salmon, and sagebrush essential to the colorful sage grouse.

34. Gifford Pinchot, *Breaking New Ground*, 252.

35. America followed the recommendation of Adam Smith, the Scottish philosopher considered the classic explicator of free market capitalism. In his seminal work, published the same year as the Declaration of Independence, Smith argued strongly for private land ownership except for lands held "for the purpose of pleasure and magnificence," which, he argued, "in a great and civilized" nation, ought to held by the national government (for him, the monarchy). Adam Smith, *An Inquiry into the Nature and Causes of the Wealth of Nations*, vol. 2 (University of Chicago Press, 1976 ed.), 349.

36. Richard Nixon, "Special Message to the Congress Proposing the 1971 Environmental Program," Feb. 8, 1971; The American Presidency Project, http://www.presidency.ucsb.edu/ws/index.php?pid=3294&st=&st1=.

37. Although often attributed to Wallace Stegner, there is no definitive evidence he coined the phrase. http://niche-canada.org/2011/10/23/who-had-americas-best-idea/.

38. E. O. Wilson, *Half Earth: Our Planet's Fight for Life* (New York and London: Liveright Publishing, 2016).

39. Enormous sums are being spent every year around the world for "ecosystem services," or economic value generated by natural systems, of the kind already being provided by the public lands in this country. See James Salzman et al., "The Global Status and Trends of Payments for Ecosytem Services," *Nature Sustainability* 1(2018):136-44; https://www.nature.com/articles/s41893-018-0033-0 (estimating that some $36–42

billion is spent annually in more than 500 active programs around the globe for such purposes).

40. The great architect and sometime Arizona resident Frank Lloyd Wright in the 1950s called the state's terrain "unique in the world," its "outlines" the "sharpest and most colorful" and its "contours" the "most picturesque," making it "destined" to become "the playground of these United States of America." F. L. Wright, Plan for Arizona State Capitol (February 17, 1957), quoted in Dean E. Mann, *The Politics of Water in Arizona* (Tucson: University of Arizona Press, 1963), 75. His description applies equally well to Utah, and he understated the matter, because foreign tourism is making the region a playground of the world.

41. See, e.g., Elizabeth MacLean, *Democracy in Chains* (New York: Viking Press, 2017); Jane Mayer, *Dark Money* (New York: Random House, 2016). The effect can be measured. The percentage of Americans who believe that the continued burning of fossil fuels would alter the climate dropped significantly in the 2000s. Naomi Oreskes and Erik M. Conway, *Merchants of Doubt: How a Handful of Scientists Obscured the Truth on Issues from Tobacco Smoke to Global Warming* (New York: Bloomsbury Press, 2010), 234, 236.

42. Senator John McCain (R-Ariz.) sounded the alarm about this developing trend shortly after the 1996 election. See McCain, "Nature is Not a Liberal Plot," *New York Times,* November 22, 1996 (questioning whether Republicans had "abandoned their roots as the party of Theodore Roosevelt," and warning against allowing "the fringes of the party to set a radical agenda" that does not represent "the mainstream of Republicans"); see also William Cronon, "When the G.O.P. Was Green," *New York Times,* January 8, 2001.

43. *Republican Platform 2016*, page 21, https://prod-cdn-static.gop.com/media/documents/DRAFT_12_FINAL[1]-ben_1468872234.pdf. Two years earlier, the Republican National Committee adopted a resolution calling on the U.S. government to transfer title to public lands to all willing western states in fulfilment of its alleged "statehood promise." https://clallamrepublicans.org/pdf_docs/RNC-Resolution-Western-States.pdf

44. See, e.g., *Landlocked: Measuring Public Land Access in the West* (Center for Western Priorities, 2013), http://westernpriorities.org/wp-content/uploads/2013/11/Landlocked-Measuring-Public-Land-Access.pdf; Kathleen McLaughlin, "Class War in the American West: The Rich Landowners Blocking Access to Public Lands," *The Guardian,*" January 21, 2018, https://www.theguardian.com/environment/2018/jan/21/public-land-battle-private-landowners-montana; Rocky Barker, "To Understand Why Billionaire Brothers Closed Off Land, Know that Texas is not Idaho," *Idaho Statesman,* August 3, 2017, http://www.idahostatesman.com/news/local/news-columns-blogs/letters-from-the-west/article165142092.html.

45. See, e.g., Timothy Egan, "Fools at the Fire," *New York Times*, August 7, 2014, https://www.nytimes.com/2014/08/08/opinion/timothy-egan-fools-at-the-fire.html.

46. In one startling example, five years ago a viewpoint overlooking the Horseshoe Bend of the Colorado River in the Glen Canyon National Recreation Area had a thousand visitors *a year*, but after it was publicized on Instagram, visitation skyrocketed to more than four thousand *per day* in 2017. https://theoutline.com/post/2450/instagram-is-loving-nature-to-death?zd=1&zi=hauydcew.

47. See, e.g., "Forest Service Wildland Fire Supression Costs Exceed $2 Billion," https://www.usda.gov/media/press-releases/2017/09/14/forest-service-wildland-fire-suppression-costs-exceed-2-billion; Sherry Devlin, "Federal Spending Bill Includes Long-Awaited Wildfire Funding Fix," https://treesource.org/news/lands/wildfire-funding/.

48. John Muir, "The Wild Parks and Forest Reservations of the West," *Atlantic Monthly* 81 (January 1898):15.

About the Author

John D. Leshy is Distinguished Professor Emeritus at the University of California, Hastings College of Law in San Francisco. Before joining the Hastings faculty in 2001, he served as solicitor (general counsel) of the Interior Department throughout the Clinton Administration, special counsel to the House Natural Resources Committee, professor at Arizona State University College of Law, associate solicitor of the Department of the Interior, and as counsel with the Natural Resources Defense Council and the Civil Rights Division of the U.S. Department of Justice. Leshy has published widely on public lands, water, and other natural resource issues, as well as on constitutional law and legal history. He has four times been a visiting professor at Harvard Law School, from which he graduated after earning an A.B. from Harvard College.